Puppies, Carrots a... ... Oh My

A True Puppy Series

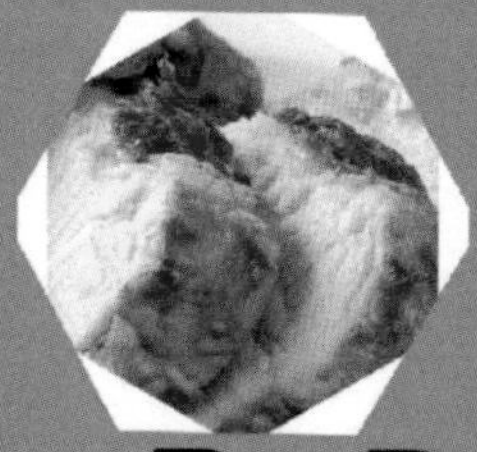

By PupKC

Published in the United States by Puppy Kids Creative LLC.

ISBN: 978-1-7334241-0-3 (Paperback)
978-1-7334241-1-0 (eBook)

The information in this book is not all inclusive. Resources to learn more are included at the end of this book. Always check with your dog's veterinarian before introducing new foods.

TABLE OF CONTENTS

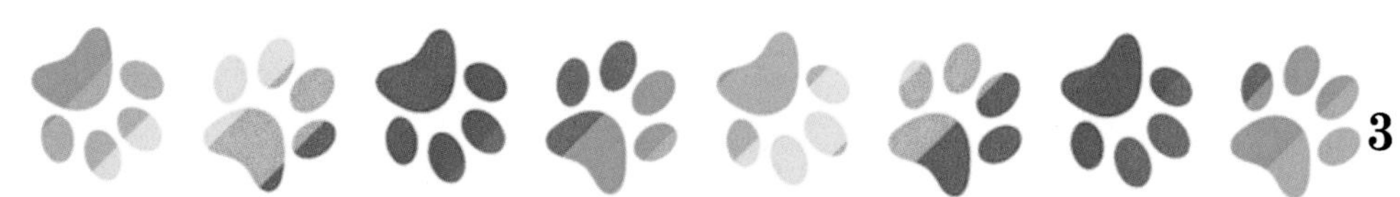

VEGETABLES

Did you know puppies and dogs don't only eat dog food? Puppies and dogs can benefit too from eating some of the same foods we eat!

Carrots

Broccoli <u>STEMS</u> only

Cucumbers

PROTEIN

Fish

Shrimp

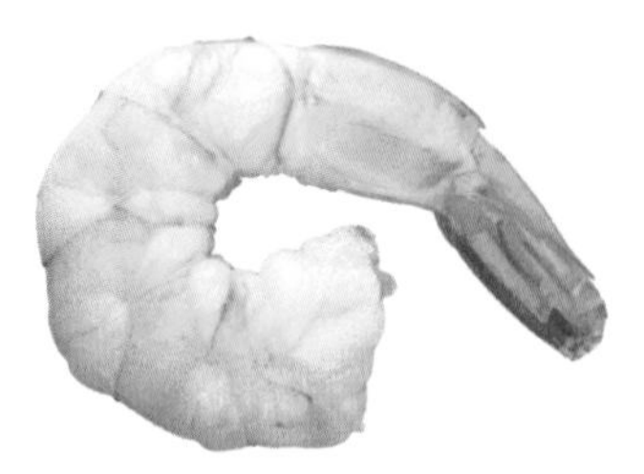

Turkey

Pork - in moderation

Tuna

Did you know?
80 percent of a dog's natural diet is meat.

FRUITS

Apples

Bananas

Blueberries

Strawberries

Peanut butter

Cashews

FRUITS

While some people foods are good for your dog, others can be very harmful. Never feed your dog the following foods...

Raisins

Grapes

Avacodos

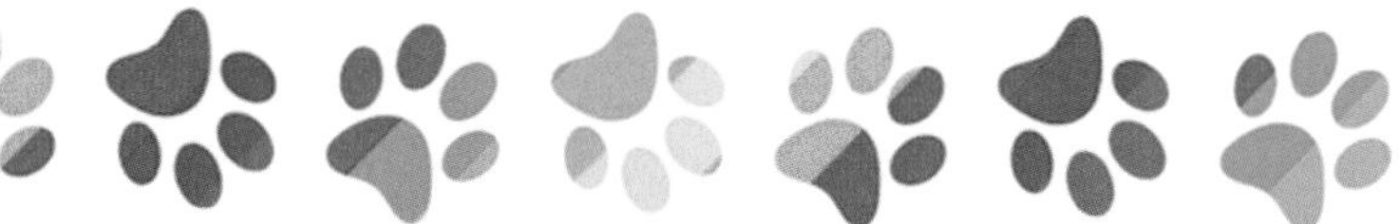
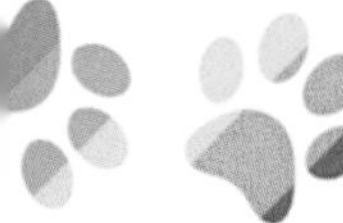

VEGGIES

Onions

Tomatoes

Tomatoe Plants

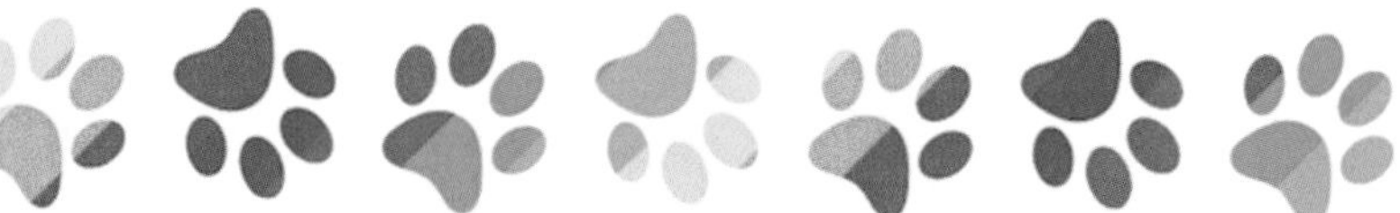
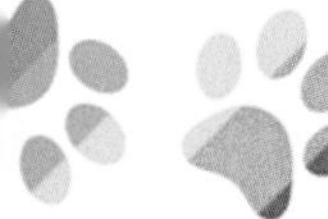
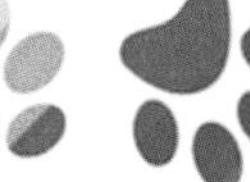

Chocolate

Sugar-free Gum

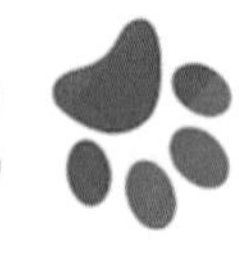

Almonds

Macadamia Nuts

Popcorn

DRINKS

Dairy

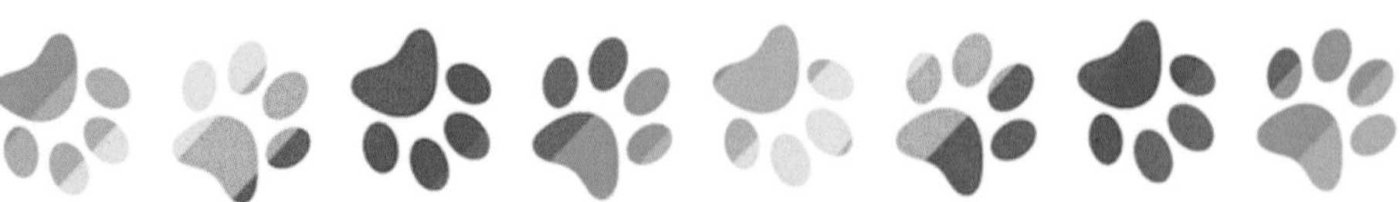

Tea

Coffee

HAPPY TIPS

A feeding routine will help your dog be happier knowing what to expect.

~ Try to feed your pups at the same time each day.

~ Put your dog's food and drink bowls in the same place everyday.

All puppies and dogs need clean fresh water, food and feeding bowls.

HEALTHY TIPS

Clean teeth and gums will help keep pups and dogs healthy:

~ Brush your pup's teeth with a soft toothbrush twice a week.

~Giving your dog raw bones and marrowbone treats will help too!

Purebred dogs may have a specialized diet.

Puppies and Dogs eat different amounts.

Puppies drink only their mother's milk for the first six to eight weeks of their life!

Puppies eat three or four times a day.

Adult dogs eat one or two times a day.

There are common household items that can be harmful if a dog eats them.

Plants like...

Poinsettias

Aloe

Ivy

Chamomile

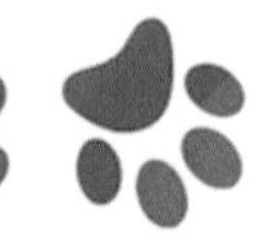

People Medicine

Cleaning Products

If you think your dog is sick or has eaten something harmful, call your veterinarian or the ASPCA Animal Poison Control Center 24-hour emergency poison hotline at 1-888-426-4435.

FOOD ALLERGIES

Did you know, like people, dogs can suddenly develop a sensitivity or allergy to food that has not previously been a problem?

Some main symptoms of food allergies are:

~ Itchy skin
~ Hair loss
~ Tail, foot and leg chewing
~ Recurrent ear infections
~ Upset stomach
~ Sneezing and wheezing
~ Behavior changes

Food allergies are often overlooked because skin problems are **assumed** to be caused by other things dogs are exposed to like fleas or pollen.

Common dog food allergens include:

~ Diary products
~ Wheat
~ Eggs
~ Corn
~ Soy
~ Whey
~ **Preservatives**
~ **Pesticides**

Food allergy causes are complex. Sometimes:

~ food **manufacturers** change ingredients
~ **substances** build up from a dog being fed the same thing over a long period of time

Tips to Help your Dog 🐶

~ Don't feed your dog table scraps
~ Purchase hypoallergenic dog food
~ Trial and error elimination diet
~ Keep a journal of reactions

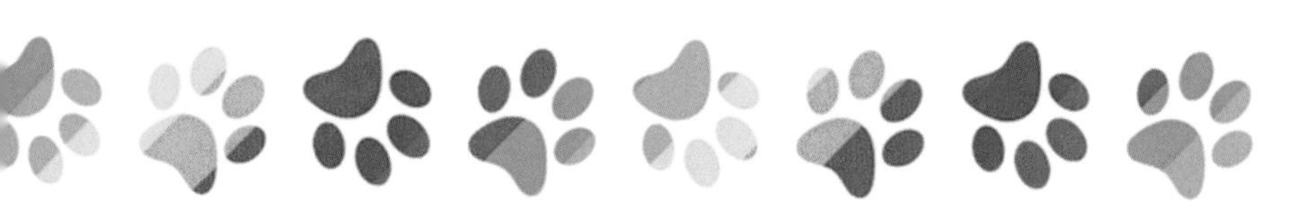

GLOSSARY

Allergy
A condition in which a person is made sick by something that is harmless to most people.

Assumed
Believed or claimed to be true or real.

Behavior
The manner in which a dog acts.

Elimination
The act or process of excluding or getting rid of.

Hypoallergenic
Having little likelihood of causing an allergic reaction

Manufacturers
A company that makes a product.

Nutrient
A substance or ingredient that promotes growth, provides energy, and maintains life.

Nutrition
The processes by which a living thing takes in and uses nutrients.

Pesticides
A substance used to destroy pests.

Preservatives
A substance added to food to keep it from spoiling.

Previously
Going before in time or order.

Purebred
Bred from ancestors of a single breed for many generations.

Recurrent
Happening or appearing again and again.

Routine
A usual order or way of doing something.

Sensitivity
The quality of a living thing to easily react to substances, state of being irritable.

Substances
A material of a certain kind.

Veterinarian
A doctor that gives medical treatment to animals.

LEARN MORE

PupKC.com

PupKC.com is an interactive educational series for kids and parents, by a real kid, pen name - PupKC.

PupKC is on a mission to prove to his mom and dad that he is ready for the fun and awesome responsibility of owning and caring for a puppy.

To learn more about puppies and dogs, visit PupKC.com.

PupKC is combining his passions for learning, creating and puppies, while helping other children learn too and giving back to the community along the way.

PupKC donates 10% of sales to local charities that have inspired his love of learning, creating and puppies.

Learn more and join in the fun at PupKC.com!

PupKC Learning Resources

These are the books and web resources PupKC read to learn and write this book.

Weblinks

American Human Association
http://www.americanhumane.org

American Kennel Club
http://www.akc.org

ASPCA
http://www.aspca.org

Woof (from PBS Program)
http://www.pbs.org/wgbh/woof/index.html

I Love Dogs
https://iheartdogs.com

Merriam-Webster Definitions for Kids
https://Merriam-Webster.com

Books

Top 10 Dogs for Kids, by Ann Graham Gaines, (Top Pets for Kids with American Human Association). Enslow Publishers, Inc. USA 2009.

Your Pet Dog, revised Edition, by Elaine Laudau. (A true Book). Children's Press an imprint of Scholastic Library Publishing, 2007.

Eyewitness DOG, by Juliet Clutton-Brock. DK Publishing, NY, NY, 2014.

The Everything Book of Dogs and Puppies, by Senior Editor Carrie Love. DK Publishing, NY, NY, 2018.

Choosing a Dog, How to Choose and Care for a Dog, by Laura S. Jeffrey. (The American Humane Association Pet Series). Enslow Publishers, Inc., US, 2013.

The Complete Dog Book for Kids, by the American Kennel Club. Wiley Publishing Inc., Hoboken, NJ, 1996.

ABOUT the AUTHOR

- PupKC, Author and Creator

I LOVE cute puppies, creative projects, learning and bowties!

I wake up at sunrise with tons of ideas for creating new projects. I began with building most of my creations from cardboard boxes and recycled materials. I have been doing this since I was three years old.

Now I am also having fun learning about puppies, creating books, videos and more!

I am grateful for my loving Mom, Dad, school teachers and community organizations that have nourished my love of learning and all of my creative projects.

I am also grateful to you. I hope you enjoyed my first book in A True Puppy Series, will share with others, visit my website to learn more about puppies and join me on my journey on my puppy mission!

PupKC.com

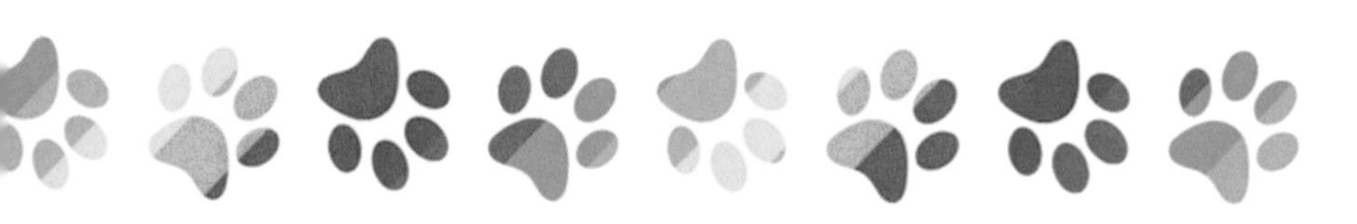

NOTES

NOTES

Made in the USA
Lexington, KY
21 November 2019